Cassy's Raw and Uncut Thoughts

Poems, Prayers, and Short Stories

by

Casandra Bailey

DORRANCE PUBLISHING CO

EST. 1920

PITTSBURGH, PENNSYLVANIA 15238

Dorrance Publishing Co
585 Alpha Drive
Pittsburgh, PA 15238
Visit our website at *www.dorrancebookstore.com*

ISBN: 979-8-8860-4367-9
eISBN: 979-8-8860-4460-7

Contents

My Heart is gone from me

This is for all of you who have lost your heart at any time during your life journey. You may have lost your heart, or it may have been stolen from you. You must know that it is yours to keep. You can get it back. You think it is gone, but it never left. Physically, your heart is still beating in your chest. You simply lost that feeling in your heart. The feeling of being alive, blood flowing, pumping emotions in and out of it. But that feeling is gone from you; it has been drained ever so slowly to make you think that you have lost it forever.

When you sit in your room, face still, wondering why you do not feel right, staring at the television and wall in a dimly lit room, sort of feeling like you could possibly be depressed, but do not know what to call it. Well, it is because you are missing a piece of you that is not connecting to your mind because it has gone away or was stolen by a thief.

My heart sometimes disconnects from the rest of my body, and I feel a sense of loss. I search for that which I lost, and I cannot find it. I search for that which is lost in this big old world. I search for that which is lost when I do not know where I am. First, I must find myself. I look for my heart under the bar stool, but only find an empty space where feet stamp in unison to the music they hear as they drink a shot of liquor while they search for their hearts. We, in unison, only find empty spaces through all of the clutter and chaos. Eventually, I found my heart as I rummaged through the trash. I threw it away with my childhood. As I searched for my emotions, I dug deep in between the plastic bags full of moldy thoughts that I consumed. My heart softly beats as I gently feed it the free breaths of easy flowing air that breezes through me.

My ears do not understand the harsh realities that pierce through them. I close them to the indescribable screeches of pains that surround me. I closed my ears to the piercing whizzes of the invisible. I kept my ears from hearing so that I did not feel the pains of the unseen murmurings and voices that were against me. There was a force field, impenetrable and thick that I formed to keep and protect myself from the pains that I have incurred. My childhood has helped me to be the strong woman that I am today with the help and guidance of Jesus.

I am thankful that I have formed that impenetrable force field as a child to keep me safe as an adult. Even though I lost myself along the way, I was not far from me because I was hidden away in my heart. I hid the true me to keep myself free. I WAS FREE FROM THE STAINED WORDS AND AC-TIONS OF THOSE AROUND ME. To remain clean, I abstained from the unseen. I ignored and tried to avoid the un-avoidances of the evils that surrounded me. It has surrounded me in the attempt to devour me and engulf my body in the ashes that are to come. I hid and ran continuously trying to search for the inner me until I found that reassurance deep within my heart. I never let it go even when I was used and mistreated. I held onto my treasure and kept it safe hidden within my forgotten heart of wonders. Jesus helped me reach deep in the hidden chambers of myself, guiding me, showing me the way in this dark maze. He lit me up and told me that everything was okay.

I am who I am because of my past

My journey has been one that I would not change
I am who I am now because of my past
I was someone who helped me become in the now
The learning process, the road has been eventful
There have been hurts, joys, pains, and loves
To remember the pieces that when put together, completes me
I am whole and will continue to patch all the rips and tears that continually
come at me to destroy my soul
I have a power within me that is greater than me
A power that is purer than I could ever be
There is a truth and invisible love that I now see
To show the world and help those who seek
There is no turning back because there is nothing for me in the past, except
my memories that will help me heal my ever-growing heart to forever last.

I am who I am because of who I was

I am all the emotions that I have accumulated over the years that I have lived so far.

I get angry, jealous, upset, sad, happy, joyous, excited, and more.

Being who I am, has brought the people to my life and the situations I have been in.

There is no changing the true me.

I have come to love myself with a kind of love that I have not felt before.

I have learned to control all those unfiltered emotions and feelings that are a part of me forever.

To have a sense of grounding when all things and people around me are fluttering like a bunch of chickens at feeding time in a chaotic bubble of their uneasiness, stress, and worries about tomorrow.

Jesus has taught me to ground myself in all things.

He is the foundation that I have rooted myself in.

My Heart Rings

God called me. God has kept His hands on me. As my light dimmed and dimmed, getting farther from Him, He was still there in the distance calling me. Patiently waiting, providing a way back to him. I turned around, squinted my blind eyes to see an ever so dim light. My God has a path laid out for me. There are many roads and choices that weave to and from that path.

How do I know I am on God's path? Am I moving within His will? Everyone has their path they must walk and run on. When we move within that path that God has so elegantly prepared for us, we see. To see... What do we see? Each person is where they are at in their life for a reason. The people they interact with, the people they observe, as well as those who they avoid, and what they avoid.

What if I am where I am supposed to be? I am supposed to learn the complicated simplicities of my Jesus. It is so hard because I have been operating on my own accord, based off of how I have built my system of truths and lies to survive. The deeper I go, the more complicated it gets because I have made a difficult system within myself to protect what I hold dear. My God dives deep within my system to fix those corruptions I have made in unrighteousness. It is okay because I did not know any better. I now know better, so it is my responsibility to work with Jesus as He sculpts me tediously from the inside out. I now know the laws of Christ and His ordinances that I must obey.

Feelings

Feelings are strong, stronger than the piercing pains of the now.

My present reminds me of who I was.

My present shows me of who I may become.

My past shows me what I must embrace to presently grow into my future.

My future has endless paths of what I can do.

When I give up control, the wants and needs of what I think I must have so that His will is fulfilled.

I am free from the restraints that society has put on me.

I had invisible bonds and chains that held me still.

I moved within an imprint that was molded just for me.

My Answer

I answered Jesus. Not with a hello, a voice heard by the ears of those around me. Not by my ears that recognize my voice when I speak. I answered God with the still voice, deep inside of me. The voice of my heart answered when He called me. My mind paid attention to the ever so soft voice of my heart. I do not recall the voice of my heart ever having a say in my life like it did that day. The voice of my heart cried out saying, "Yes, Lord, I am here." My mind meditated on that unheard voice of my heart. My mind cried because the voice of my heart finally opened and spoke the unspeakable utterances never said. Or, even if the voice of my heart did utter, I really did not pay as much attention as I should have over the years like I did that day.

Remembrance. I stayed in that moment for as long as I could. The touch of the Father was magnified on me and in me at that moment. I did not want it to end, but I knew eventually that feeling would pass away like the beginning and the ending of a flower blooming in its' season. So, instead of forgetting that feeling, I remembered everything, as much as I could about it. The touch of the Father, how could I forget it? I stayed in that moment of love. The voice of my heart and of my mind still remembers many years later. I was surrounded by the beauty of Father inside and out. The inner me was changed forever from that moment of remembrance.

The Help That I Need

I am falling deep into the black abyss.

A dark and deep nothingness that will swallow me as I fall deeper.

I once was, to be no more because I am swallowed up as though I am nothing.

Then I look up into the deep abyss and wave my hand across as if to summon for help.

The help that I need comes to me in the form of all the planets, big and small.

Their size and colors vividly fly closer to me.

The planets line up one on top of the other vertically and form a rope for me to climb up from the deep.

I climb up fearless because I get the help that I need to stay alive.

As I am to the top of the ladder, I wave my hand across to tell the planets to go back to where they first were.

I stare up as they fly across the deep abyss, and they twinkle as they get far from me.

The help that I need comes to me.

Realization

The realization of the help that I need.
It is the help that I have.
What I had all this time.
To be sorrow as the sorrows interrupt me and surround me daily trying to tackle me away from the realization that I have.
A push, a pull in this direction and that.
A fall, a stumble, only to fall back down again.
A realization that I get back up even after that hard trip to the ground.
The dirt in my face as I wipe grass off my cheek.

I lay in the dirt on my back with my face to the sky.
Staring up into the unseen waters that surround me.
Wondering what is next and asking the why's.
Why am I dirt laying in the dirt only to fear the dirt?
A death of life realized.

Lava that Flows

The lava continues to flow as it burns everything up that is in its path in a flash.
What was is gone in an instant.
The heat is so hot that whatever it is that crosses its path will be gone and
will be no more.
The memory fades away as quick as a memory can be processed.
Burning what is; Heating the deep desires to never become because the lava
that flows.
The lava that flows out of the depths rages as it consumes everything that it
touches.
Wanting to not be in that path, yet it is coming right at me.
What do I do? I continue to move away from it until I cannot no more.
Yet, there is a way out as I keep it moving, but I must be fast.
Do not turn back as the lava flows.
I am frantic. We must leave now. Forget everything, but we must go.
What I value is in the path of the lava, but I must let it go.
Those things that are of true value will already be where I will go.

I sweat
Toss and turn, I stir
Roll around
Armpits sweaty
Body heavy
Water beads on my face
There is something about this space, Relax and chill

Feel the Heat

The heat touches my skin as I back away quickly.

It gets hotter the closer that it gets.

If the heat gets any closer, I will melt away in an instance.

I will be as a vapor.

The mist of heat vapors rises from my skin as I back away.

The harder I back away, the slower I go.

To fight with a fight that I cannot win.

The harder I fight, the weaker I AM.

I scream silently for the Great I AM to save me from this flame of fire that is unquenchable.

The heat rises from my skin as I yell inside myself for the Everlasting Water to save me from this scorching fire.

I start to disappear very slowly. My whole being flakes away as the fire engulfs me from the inside out.

My chest rises and fall as I breath heavy breaths of uncertainty that I will make it out alive from this nightmare.

The realization that death forever is a possibility that scares me straight into existence.

Existence of obedience changes me for eternity.

Lava

My mouth is dry. I swallow my spit hoping it will help. Of course not. It briefly wets my throat, then I thirst again.

My lips are chapped, and it is an effect of the fire within me burning, trying to scorch my whole being from the inside out.

The fire within me that I used to feed, the Lord puts it out with His living water, quenched for eternity.

This present state of my being reminds me of what I could be as immortal.

The dry, cracked, dead worm that will be forever. The pain-stricken worries of a scream on fire that will never be put out.

The reminders of my will. The workings of a selfish woman who cares less of herself than herself.

A woman who cares more for the temporary releases of what has potential for eternal life.

Does my inaction result in a change of circumstances? When I choose to not do something instead of doing something, this ultimately results in a decision being made. The cycle of being broke, the cycle of being broken, ends.

Bonfire Heat

Imagine standing in front of a bonfire and you feel the heat rise on your skin.
You step away very quick, as quickly as the fire hit you.
Now, if you could not stand that heat, what makes you think you can live
immortal as a worm that will burn for eternity?
There will be weeping and gnashing of teeth.

Two-Edged Sword

A two-edged sword has been sharpened.
If you are not careful and as are as the foolish, then that two-edged sword
will become a tongue.
To say a word with a snake's tongue, to whisper lies so sweet.
A taste that lingers.
A slither to hear not with my ears.
Get away from me Satan.

Words so powerful.
Say a syllable next to a syllable that when spoken shuts it down.
The words that you read, the words that you hear, speak.

Wake up

Coming to the realization of the God in me.
I fall asleep like I do every day, to wake up from a dream within a dream.
Realizing that I was still sleeping.
I was asleep to the true meanings of what surrounds me.
Why do I have to wake up to people staring at me?
Knowing something about me that I do not even know about myself yet.
You do not know me and what I go through.
You only see what I show you.

The Emerald Head

Sandra woke up and saw a very little fairy flying around her room. She chased it around the room until she gently cupped it in both of her hands. The fairy gave her a gift that was only hers to have.

Sandra's emerald dress flowed down the aisle like a fountain, shining with all elegance and beauty. Her emerald headdress shone the brightest of all the heads as she walked about. It floated above her head and turned whenever she turned. Her emerald headdress never left from above her head.

One day, Sandra woke up to get dressed, but her emerald dress and headdress were nowhere to be found. She walked out to the community, and she saw another girl wearing her dress and headdress, but it did not flow and shine on this other girl as it did on her. It was a plain dress and headdress that was a bland grayish color, and was not near as beautiful as its original form. The girl walked about with this man as though he was hers, but he will never be her emerald head like with Sandra.

Sandra waited patiently until her head came back to her. Once he was back, her emerald dress and headdress returned to its beautiful flowing form. It shone the brightest of all the other heads. It was hers to have and to hold forever. Her head flowed down the aisle like a fountain, shining with all elegance and beauty like it never lost its shine.

A Single Thread

A single thread can result in a beautiful dress that I wear as my crown floats above my head. My back straight and feet rooted firmly on the ground. Arms swaying quietly by my side as I continue to walk forward.

Clothes I Wear

The clothes I wear are the extension of pieces of me.
Pieces of who I can be, who I am not, as well as who I want to see.
What I own may be of my choosing or given to me as a gift from another.
The endless options of colors and styles that best suits the child of a mother.

All the colors that shine on me
Rainbow vibrates of who I will be
Shirt and a skirt sewed not by chance
Twirl and twist of a special dance

Battle for old lifestyle

A cycle that I started to begin again:
The person I was emerged back with a mission to remain the same.
The battle got real.
I saw myself beginning to make the same choices and decisions I once made before.
But I was a new person in Christ.
I knew that I needed to make different choices.
 I must change my course and not trust the old me to help me as I become the new me.
I had to trust.
I must trust in the Lord and not me because it was evident that I made some wrong decisions based off where I was.
Based off my past decisions, I have made behavioral and thought changes.
I was fighting for my life.
I was fighting for change.

Battle between Light and Darkness

I was in the middle of this battle between light and darkness. I was the battle between light and darkness. I was aware of it as it was happening in me with every choice and action that I made in my life during this time. There was a big war for my heart. I tried to choose light in everything that I did. If I felt a change in me that was going towards the darkness, I changed my direction.

It was a flicker of evil or darkness and my mental changed; I knew that was not who I was or who I wanted to be. The light and darkness flickered back and forth between my thoughts and my choices. I did not like how I would change for the darkness. My thoughts, my expressions, my feelings would change, and I was aware of that ever-changing battle war within me.

Deep down inside I knew that I was light, and when that darkness overcame me, it was not me. I was a beam of light waiting for God to touch me to brighten me up to my full capacity. The darkness was around me and tried to come through me. The light was stronger, and I allowed the light to fully encompass within and around me. I literally shook off the darkness like it was a bad thought that I had to clear from my mind.

To keep the light within me, I studied the Word of God. I wanted it to stay with me forever and always. I never wanted the light to leave me again. I felt how it was to be dark and I did not like it. I knew what it meant to be evil and wanted to be far from it. I chose to stay close to God. I chose to remain in Him as He remained in me. He is my light and my shine.

Experiencing Change
Why did this specific experience occur?

I considered why I went through this specific experience. I asked, "why did it happen to me?" There is this change that is occurring within me and around me. I thought about it and the answer was that I wanted it to happen. There was this desire deep inside of me that drew this experience to me. I allowed my perceptions, thoughts, and behaviors to be challenged. I gave up control of trying to be in control of everything.

One thought seed grew, and I cultivated it. That seed sprouted and grew. My strongly held beliefs and ways of life I gave up to God. I allowed Him to work in me, mold me, and completely strip my mind of those programmed thoughts and behaviors. As I did this, He gave me time after time, mistake after mistake to get it as close to right as was in me. He gave me time and space to get closer to Him as my ability allowed me to.

Trials

How will our relationships turn out as we go through those fiery trials of God?

I am in my trial as I go living for God.

As my strength, He is guiding me, allowing me, providing for me in a way out of the prison, the slavery of this world.

The prison of my mind has trapped me within the illusions that blind me to the truth and the unrealities and invisible forces that bind me.

Jesus, the blood of Jesus breaks me free from those bondages.

The invisible chains that keep me held within a dark painful endless pit of misery, pain, hurts, and tears of death. He became all of that for me.

Where there is one searching, there is more.

There is this feeling that there is more out there.

There is something deeper inside, festering, bubbling, trying to find an escape.

There is more, deep within you wanting to explode.

Be calm, stay grounded, and focused.

Find your lane and stay in that path allowing Jesus to be your guide on that path.

Get to know your one true guide.

There is need for only one guide, Jesus

A Way of Humbling Me

The Lord has a special way of humbling. How He humbles me is a humbling experience indeed.

He brings my iniquities to the surface of my being. Who I am was who I thought I was until that iniquity within that is hiding breaks through and scares me.

The reality of finding who I really am is humbling. With the Light shining in the darkest secrets of my soul. Bringing to light what I carefully hidden away deep within the crevices.

Cracks and tiny hiding places for any sin to sneak off again. Until I shine the light and the shadows of what it illuminates.

An injured me retreats deep within, to recuperate with hopes to resurface and live.

To live a life without boundaries has weakened my soul. I detached from those feelings and memories that held me down. That kicked and punched me to the center of who I am.

The humbling experience allowed me to live with boundaries, but to still be free from those things that hold me back. What holds me back to keep me from living free as I am meant to be.

My Surroundings

My external is dirty, so I must clean it up. But how to wipe the everchanging? First, go internal.

What do I view as something I do not want or like? Around me; specifically in my surroundings.

How to decide when enough is enough.

The perpetual, inevitable, endings.

The end shows in the beginning.

The undeniable truths that show the internal you.

Who you have become by the accumulation of your decisions.

What a man is, who a man is, shows in his heart. This overflows into his mouth with a sail full sailing, moving to and fro on the waters. This is the truths of the word and every man his own parts.

My surroundings are the external of who I really am; What is and what is to come. Waiting for the yays and nays that will help me to determine the direction that I will go.

Decisions and actions are made by my reactions. My mind thinks for my body to move. A constant flow that refreshes. The very sweet-smelling savor that is full of a great essence.

Her Identity

Who she knew to be herself; All what made her who she recognized day by day when she looked herself in the mirror, was gone. She did not know who stared back at her with those same eyes that she has looked at ever since she knew it was her.

She does not know which way the road leads because she has never been there before. She is scared because what if the way she goes returns her back to where she started.

She does not know that place. To be in a spot every day and barely even know. Trying to recognize the unrecognizable. Trying to understand her space. How can I be who I am, when all around me tests my nerves to help me become who I am?

Increase my ability to grow Lord.

Your perception and another person's perception of you while you are perceiving.

A Regular Woman

No one comes to the Father, except by through Me.

I am a regular woman, finding my place in this world.

We tend to hide who we are so that we can become who we know deep inside who we truly are.

The time it takes can last a lifetime when the real you present itself.

Oh, if the worlds time was on my time. If only it would give me the space that I need as I search.

To back up 6 feet away from me, as I shine my brightness that God graciously has given me.

Jesus, I thank You for revealing to me who I was for you. My weakest times have shown so much strength when You are there. The greatest lessons I have learned for others to share.

My internal environment seems so small to be a huge part in who I am today.

It is contained in my physical body.

Our senses are extended to the external.

I am more than my internal.

I am what appears to be.

When I truly met me

She is running like a bull with her head down, horns out.

All she sees is red.

The thoughts of a levelheaded woman are completely gone and have been replaced with a deep-seated anger that erases all and any calm demeanor that she is known to have at any given moment.

 Where did this hate come from?

It comes from the external words of her environment that she internally harvested within her weak and fragile body.

She is already dying from the fact of simply being alive. Her "aliveness" radiates a glow that others envy.

Other's scratch, hit, bite, and scream at her sweet innocence.

They made her see red.

They made her see the reds of the emotions that rise from her inner heart.

Her mind is missing the valve that "shuts off in case of an emergency" type of event.

I must remember the heat that rises from my cheeks, up my face, to my forehead.

The inner stomach, lungs, and heart feel the rages rising within.

That woman is me!

I am not fighting

I am not fighting the girl in the street.
I am not yelling at the guy on the sidewalk.
I am fighting and yelling at myself.
The inner workings of what irks me, bubbles up as it reaches the reasonings
of my mind.
Forget about growth.
Forget about maturing.
What matters is me getting my point across with these pointless back and
forth of fighting and yelling that have no real substance.

Lies

For the father of lies inputs his lies into my head.

My words manifest those lines of stirrings that I incubated and took care of, then decided to speak it as my truth.

I know who my enemy is. I then listened to his lies.

I became those lies by allowing those lies to grow in my head.

Then all that manifests are those lies first said.

The enemy strategizes, trying all angles to see where I am the weakest.

If the enemy sees a weak spot, he will press on that wound until I would squirm in agony like an injured worm.

I trip my own self up. I tangle my own feet in what the enemy has laid out for me.

All the enemy had to do was lay deceit and treachery right at my feet for me to walk on it and stumble.

The enemy wants you to play their game. If they act like a high school child, they will play high school games.

The manipulation and deceit are real and will be on that level. Do not play those games because you are growing and maturing spiritually.

No Eating Disorder, but Spiritual Order

No, I did not have an eating disorder, I was having Spiritual order. The order of Christ and His laws. All that I was, had to be stripped away to become a new creature in Christ.

I held on for dear life. I fought for all I ever knew. I protected myself from the pains that I buried deep inside. I fought for that girl that I had become; the me that was in the now.

I calmly called her to say that it was okay. I softly said her name as not to push her farther away.
I reached out my hand waiting for her to reach back. Looking into her eyes with the love of a father to his child, saying I love you and everything is on track.

Those experiences were extreme at first. I was being taught and then disciplined on what I have learned from Christ.

I admit that I can be stubborn. That is just who I have always been. For God to fulfill His will in me, I must give up that stubbornness for understanding, knowledge, and fear.

Oh, what I have gained. Not riches or honor, but the true gift of God which is life. I can truly be happy with what I currently have. All of that complaining and whining must go and never come back.

What is in the dark will come to the light. Are you ready for what will shine in your life?

Do not be afraid of your darkest memories. The light will take them away with a flicker of a flame. To see your sins as they emerge will be the thing that you fear the most. Just like your childhood worst memory that you buried deep inside. When your fear presents itself, only look to the Lord and say You are Hosts of hosts who take my sins away.

When I am here, I become what is thy will. The light that brightens up my darkness. The light that brightens up the darkness. The shift that occurs as the rise and sun sets of each day. From today to tomorrow, back to today. The moving forward seasons and times of the now.

I have this hunger deep within the pit of my stomach. A feeling that causes my whole being to change ever so slightly. The reactions that occur are directly connected to the reaction before it. The hunger feelings in my stomach make a gargling noise as if to say aloud that a process is occurring. It reached my esophagus as it rose to reach its destination. The noise said "ting" as if the bell rings at dinner time. My throat said "ting" as the process continues. A reaction connected to a reaction from before it. My ears hear a sound, my body is as it is. It is such a subtle thing, that smallest flicker that scares you. It is a flicker from that light you were in, to that darkness that reminds you of your worst fears in life.

A change within a change. That while the darkness surrounds you, the light will always remain Within you is the flame that stays lit when Jesus lights you up. For eternity can be dark or light, depending on you. Your choices come from within your deepest desires. Those that come alive as you breathe a breath, then another breath, the spirit of your being. The dark and light coexist at the same time. A balance to the order of things. The flicker of one flame as it lights up your surroundings. It is only one small ball of heat that burns the wick with a flick. What I once shattered came together again. A precious stone, colorful.

Mermaid in a Cage

When the cage is unlocked, but I do not realize it. I sit as a mermaid in a cage. A wonder of wonder that amazes people. Oh, how I seem to be a mermaid free, when I am locked in this invisible cage that surrounds me like that water that flows constantly.

No key is needed because the lock is unlocked. No key is needed because I am the key. I see what I see, which is something that surrounds me. The claustrophobic feeling when I am not claustrophobic, of being locked up every day.

The secrets that hold me and bind me to this non-materialistic cage that suffocates me daily.

The hidings and running, as if someone is chasing me when there is nobody but my reflection in the mirror looking back at me. My eyes see me. My eyes look back at the blank stares of who I thought I was in the present. It is like time rewinds and starts over again. To be trapped again in the endless cycles of being a mermaid in a cage. The wonder of wonders. The beautiful mysterious talents of a mermaid standing still as if the cage that surrounds her, when the only cage is her mind that binds her.

Break free of the stainless-steel thing that you think is there. Break free of the invisible chains that hold you down. Those chains that break with a breeze of the wind that passes by it so gracefully.

Multidimensional

What was
What is
What is to come
What would be
What could be
What should be
When?
Just when you think that is it.
Wait there is more.

One question leads to an answer, which in turns leads to another question. It builds upon and builds, cycling through to the complete picture.

A piece to the whole, just when you think you have the whole. Whoa, wait. Another piece introduces itself that presents another answer.

It builds upon builds, starting at the foundation. A structure so concrete, it bricks with wonders shining ever so bright.

Emotions I Feel

I have felt alone when surrounded by people. I felt broke when I had a job working 40 hours a week. I have felt homeless even when I had a roof over my head. Those feelings were my internal breaking forth introducing itself to me.

How could I feel those things? Was something wrong with me? Of course, something was wrong with me. I would not feel that way for nothing. My feelings matter. If they did not matter, I would not feel in the first place.

Sometimes I want to scream from the pains I have. Other times I want to crawl up in a little ball and lay in the dark under my blankets with nobody interrupting me. I value my silent moments and calm tomorrows because the next moment and next day may not be the same.

What is with the uncertainties? Can I get a definite relaxing time without the petty interruptions?

If I could know for sure that my day would occur without the surprise headaches and low yelling of what may come.

Timeless

I ask about time to make sure that I am at that time.

To understand the current events, to make connections in that time.

I was back to the future.

It was futuristic.

I am in the present viewing the future.

I am the future looking at how it was when I was in my present viewing my future, which is the past now.

I presently am present with what is happening to me now.

The past events are currently relevant.

The relevance of what I now experience.

This is what those in the past wished with all their hearts to be a part of, which was to come eventually.

Time has no boundaries.

It is realer than your very small reality.

The unseeing element, that goes through you and me.

One Confined Area

This small, confined area scares me. It reminds me of my youth time fears and adulthood shadows.

I retreat away to the screams and kicks with far away eyes closed terrors.

What was, what is, and what could be scares me.

The endless what ifs that stare back.

Mindless thoughts that betray all that could be.

I remember this small, confined area that brings me back to the realities of what presents as my mind expands.

The expansion of the reaction from the interaction between us.

We live in this one confined area. With two minds that are a wonder of wonders that God gives.

To show His beautiful gifts. To be the God of. Forever He lives.

This small, confined area reminds me of what was, what is, and what is to come.

What is of my brother and sister, I am also responsible of.

Time and time again

I have been here before.
What's different?
What's the same?
The cycle of everything continues,
Leaves and comes back again.
A fresh,
Renewed.
Your love,
It's true.

The reality of this time warped world

People can't even tell time,
What is infinite?
How can one bottle it up and slap a price on it?
One clock says 7:03,
Another says 7:05.
What is this hypocrisy?
Is time time, or is it not?
I know time is neither the former nor the latter,
But if you're going to try to contain it,
Please be consistent.
Time is free.
Time is open air.
It's meant to be everlasting.
An infinite, ever moving, invisible,
Yet visible, if you look close enough, gift.
It has a bow on it,
Your name is on it.
Keep your mind on it.
Never moving.
Always stopped,
Never stopped,
Always moving.
It's one in the same,
Same difference.

Manifestation

We each have made the choices in our lives up to our present.
Even our future?
The question is, what to do from that moment forward?
What choices am I to make that will affect my unwoven future?
My past choices became my present and my present choices will be my future.
All my choices have already been made,
even the ones not yet made.
How can this be you ask?
This is because of who I am and what I have manifested in my life.

I am for my brother

One leads to another.

One thing flows to the following.

When this connects to that, I am for my brother.

To protect, to reflect on the ins and outs, the is and was of the tomorrows.

My thoughts become what they are, to think the words spoken to me.

These things do not seem real because I found my tree.

What was gone from me, I found again.

What was once me is me once more.

To be is to be, to say is to say.

Doing what is needed today.

I am not responsible for just myself, but for those whom God appointed me responsible for.

My actions do not only affect me, but also those around me.

My actions will affect those directly connected to me, whether at home, work, or in passing.

I must think of all outcomes according to Gods will,

and make the best possible decision for the collection of minds.

The Lord orchestrates instruments around me.

My sound mixes well with others,

while my sound sometimes does not mix well with another.

I must find that connection and synchronize with those whom I am unsynchronized with.

The vibes do mix well.

Why would I want to remain unsynchronized with those who I am always around?

I will not allow such bad music to interrupt my sound.

I will find that note in you that plays well with my note.

Obscured Darkness

Darkness can appear bigger and scarier than it really is. Have you ever saw the shadow of a bag and hot sauce bottle sitting on the kitchen room table? The angle when the light hits it, obscures it. They look bigger than they really are. That can scare a person. When the thing that you fear the most is not a thing that you should fear because of the simple appearance of it.

When I was a child, I feared our basement. It was huge, dark, and cold, and that was the spot I had to go to wash and dry my clothes. I had to get it done myself because everyone else had their own personal loads to do. I would open the door and stand on the very top steps, hoping that this time when I go to switch on the light, it would turn on. Of course not.

I begin to slowly walk down the creaky steps as the light from the kitchen gets farther away and the darker it gets. As I walk into the darkness, my eyes are trying to adjust so that I can see what is in front of me. As soon as I hit the bottom step, I breath, then bolt as fast as I can to the washer so I can quickly turn that tiny not so bright lightbulb on that is hanging over the washer.

I am going as fast as I can to get my clothes in, turn the washer on, and bolt right back on up those steps until I must come to the basement to switch my clothes over to the dryer. This time I have that tiny little light on. Out of courtesy, I make sure that I turn the tiny light off when I am done drying my last load. I look around, turn off the light, and run up those stairs.

The thing I feared the most, I had to conquer alone.
Everybody was too busy fighting
their own monsters to help me fight my monsters in the basement.

I Inadequately Love Others

I have learned how to inadequately love others.
I learned this by the love of those around me.
They learned that sort of love kind of giving and taking.
I wonder if he recognizes what makes me who I am?
Does he recognize that I am still her that he fell in love with?
Unless...he doesn't see me as that person anymore.
If I am supposed to grow in the LORD and be transformed into a new creature,
how am I to stay that same exact person who you first met?
I am still that same person that is simply growing in the Lord.
What does growth look like?
What does a woman/man of God look like?
How are we supposed to balance our own individual wants and needs and
satisfy our husband's/wife's wants and needs at the same time?
There is a balance to this that we must work together on.
It takes two willing participants, a husband, and a wife, to make that happen.
We must work within the will of God to achieve this outcome.
Do you recognize me?
I recognize you.
I remember the love of my life.
How could I ever forget?
Look into my eyes and remember.
Am I who I have always been now?
He said to never change.
I said okay, meaning it deep within me.
Wanting to always be who he fell in love with.
If I lose that part of me, he will drift away from me on the river of come and
goes in this life.
To never look back,
To never remember me.

As this transformation occurred,

I changed.
Who I was, I grew into who I was supposed to be.
God started to work in me
To teach me.
Who am I to tell God no when He calls me?
Even though this means that I may lose the very essence of my love demon-
strated to him.
We did not know what to expect.
Who really knows what they will become when nobody has taught them
about the process?
Teach me how to teach Father.

Who I was, was not who I was.
It was merely who I was.
A glimpse of the many me's
The side of me that was unholy.
He saw a virtuous woman that I could be.
Even through the shell that I built to protect me.

My Sister and I

My sister and I
We always shared a room
We shared a womb, shared a room
Not the womb at the same time
But were birthed back-to-back
14 months
Teared apart
Separated
Brought back together
Family ties
Even as adults
We shared the womb
Shared a room
Moved back in with momma
I moved out the room
She moved in that womb
Close again
Yet so far apart
We are birthed back-to-back
The cries that echo
I still hear the cries the baby has for its mother
The umbilical cord is cut
It's broken
The pains of birthing
From momma to child, from child to child, back to momma again
The Very Essence of You

Relationship

Our relationships define who we currently are.

If you are not satisfied with your current relationships, then make some adjustments.

To those whom I have a relationship with, I have been by your side as you feel the burning hurts of life.

When you cannot breathe because the very breath that comes from your chest hurts.

The very essence of you disgusts your inner self.

Why do you feel that way?

The important matter is that you are needed alive.

The very breath you breathe brings to life the things that are dying around you.

Look around, they need you.

Your mental capabilities allow you to include a lot more people in your atmosphere than the average.

Make sure that your environment is not toxic like those who enter it.

Neutralize their negative energy with your energy, God fearing, and positive.

Hair

What do the curls on my head say about me?
They can be the wavelengths of my reality that make me to be.
The spirals of my extended nerves help me to navigate this plane of existence.
I do not manipulate.

I allow all information that comes to me and thru me to remain in its purest
and raw form so that
I can hear the Word of God and His TRUTHS.

What are those things that I absorb?
You wipe away my tears here in the physical realm. Lord, You spiritually
wipe my tears away.
To be able to recognize the here and in the now.
To You O' Lord, I bow.
I read your words and truth, I become your living word and truth.
I am your testimony.
To live in poverty, sick to my stomach, not because I am hungry,
but because I fear the unknown and what will happen to me next.
I am learning how to release the sickness that so engulfs the deepest parts of
my existence.

I Got One in the Chamber

Everything has led to this moment.
A choice must be made, and it is now.
The wheels in my mind are turning.
Burning a mile a minute.
Ticking while my hand is on the chamber.
The chamber of my heart ticks as the tocks moves forward on the clock.
Every second passes and I wonder about the unknown.
There is this peace that I graciously thanked God for.
A peace that I would not have without Him.
The peace I asked for, believing, I received.
Click clack as the hands move forward on the clock.
A tock, a tick, a blink of the eye and only a second has passed by.

My Everyday Throne is a Toilet Bowl

Let me go sit on my throne has a whole new meaning. I must wonder daily of my throne sitting and how it is such a basic thing to do. It is a thing that I cannot ignore, even for a day.

The bathroom has so much activity in it from day to day. As much as one person uses it for a toilet break, warm bath, teeth brushing, and more. After all of that, the bathroom is just a bathroom that needs to be cleaned.

I think of a saying, "let me go to my throne room," and I make a deep connection. As the created, I must recognize that my creator sits on His Holy Throne above all. How dare I make any comparison to His righteous throne.

A Failing Heart

My HEART FAILS. Yet, it stills beats day to day. A beat that is out of sync with the rest of my body; a beat that is more like a tick tock as the hands continues to move forward every second on the clock that I watch on the wall. I stare at the hands that move in a slow continuous movement forward. This reminds me that every forward movement that I make is slow, but it is definite until my heart fails me once more. My heart fails as I go day to day doing my daily routines, switching it up every now and then. I may go to the store or drive a different way. I have a failing heart that yearns to beat strong to the sounds of His whispers. I missed a beat yesterday. It was more like my blood pumping in and out of my veins and then rushed to my head to give me that lovely temple thumping feeling. Then, I need to lay down and close my eyes to the ever so bright light and loud sounds that rush at me at the same time kind of feeling. Time flowing as my heart beats and fails day by day. My brain is thumping as my heart beats harder. The blood tries to flow through my veins, systematically pumping. My heart fails me once again. My mind remembers when my heart was young and healthy; Running a mile in ten minutes with energy to run another mile in ten minutes. My heart remembers how I used to be compared to how I am now. I have aged as time continued to move forward on that clock on the wall. That clock with its' hands moving ever so slowly. One tick a second; one tock a minute; one hour has passed. I look and time has moved forward as my heart fails me.

I didn't think about my heart much as I was younger. My mind was on the present moment in my life, my youth, my friends, my current feeling, and emotions at that time. Time has been good to me. Time has allowed me to keep moving forward as I watch the hands on the clock tick again.

Time beat in unison with my heart as I breathed in deeply with each breath God has given me. My heart fails me as time remembers me. Time remembers being in rhythm with my heart as soon as it beat.

That first time my heart started was the beginning of me. Time rejoiced when my heart came alive! There was another heart to join in on the time that was to be. I am alive even though my heart fails me day to day. Yet, it still beats as time moves on. I thank Yah for this life that He allows me. Thank you.

My heart skipped a beat yesterday. It Jumped and felt as though it missed the ledge and went over. There was silence during that skip, and it scared me. I searched for that lost moment in time but could not find it. It passed by within a skip and did not come back to me. I remember when it happened but did not feel it. That feeling of a heart that failed me was all that lingered on. The lingering of what once was, angers me because I know there was something there, but is gone now; that something that I wanted to feel is gone. My heart fails.

Gifts from God

Your heart is close to mine.
It beats in my chest where a hole once was.
You breathe the breath of life into every one of us,
so that we can worship and praise You Lord.
My chambers are ready for you.
There is a place for you in my heart.
Thank you for meeting me heart to heart.

Instruments

You have different speeds.
Each speed depends on the phase of your life.
I ask myself, what are those things that I must learn at this exact time in my life?
I am within the Lords will.
Tells me a lot about how I learn as a willing instrument of God.
I flow with others,
not to bump them or interject in their tunes,
but to remain in harmony with God,
with myself,
and with them all at the same time.
We are Gods instruments.
When I am working within His will be done on earth as it is in heaven, I am operating, working
day and night doing His will.

I am living within the confinements of God's laws.
Orchestration of everything
The synchronicities of different sounds,
different instruments,
different faiths.

The Length of Time

Who are you?

A loved one?

A stranger?

A friend?

An enemy?

Nobody?

I count the seconds,

minutes,

hours,

days,

months,

years,

ions?

The length of time, who knows, only God.

My lessons and tests occur with each passing breath.

Determining what I must learn to get to where I must be in a future point in my life,

(Be it present) or is it to get me where I must be in the future for the will of God to work perfectly in me?

Or does it determine how important that lesson or test will be to your overall will of God?

What do these tests and trials that I go through say about me?

I am going through the fiery trials of God. I am in my trial as I go living for God.

As my strength, He is guiding me, allowing me, proving me, providing for a way.

The prison of my mind has trapped me within the illusions that blind me.

The unrealities and invisible forces that trap and bind me.

Synchronicity

Jesus, the blood of Jesus breaks me free from those bondages.
The invisible chains that keep me held within a dark painful endless pit of
misery, pain, and tears of death.

He became all of that for me and for you.

I am primitive to the technologies of the world.
I have lived within a time that stood still.
A time that moved at a different speed than technology.
Trying to remain untouched with the stains of the impurities.
I am in a time capsule that has preserved me for the Lord
Oh, how great it is to live without the stains of the ever-changing evolving
ways of man.
To have a basic instinct that has kept me safe within the borders of my mind
and it was embedded deep within my soul.
The unknown can be dangerous, or the unknown can lead me to a God that
is alive forever more and loves me as His child.

Who knows how God will orchestrate it?
All that I know is that God's orchestra is the
most beautiful, pure, and holy synchronicity ever!!

The Movement

See how the pieces move ever so fluid
Oh no, that instrument sounds off, we need to fix it
The sound that it emits must needs a tune up

I stand in a room full of people and feel that I am alone
Even though I am not alone
The see-through stares, the nothing talks
Words that evaporate in the air before it reaches my head
To mix and mingle with the electricity that awaits to transport the unsaid
My eyes see the blank, emotionless eyes looking back at me
To have eyes that take on the most, burden heavy energies, only to release
them back into the invisible for recycling
The neutral, untouched, invisible energy that floats around me
The waiting to come to me as a current of electricity moves through me

The Rhythm of Life

The unknown I embrace.
I embrace what I do not know.
What I don't know, I fear.
I fear the Lord more.
I fear the Lord.
Fear is the beginning of knowledge.
I am able to be in the present.
I pull from the past.
I see the future in our very present moment of what we could be.
To know the past,
To experience the future.
Becoming what once was, now.
To know glimpses of future,
Seeing what will happen.
Seeing if the choices we make now are within God's will.
To fear the unknown because it hurts my present being,
Only to bear these growing pains of what once was,
that is no more.
I was an infant who grew to become an adult.
Working within God's law to transform again.
To become His holy and righteous instrument.

Ultimate Conductor

You, God are the Ultimate Conductor.

To be able to orchestrate the movement of all things living in a way that benefits all life is beauty, true beauty.

My Jesus is all consuming Beauty.

You are true beauty and Great in Majesty Father.

Thank You.

I love You with all my heart, my body, my mind, my strength, and all my soul.

I will be able to recognize the sound of the Lord.

My body responds to sound in a way as if that sound travels thru me.

The sound resonates within my organs as it travels.

This is the way of the LORD.

My heart feels the crinkle of paper.

Oh, how much more my heart is to feel when the Lord moves me according to His will.

The synchronicities of our bodies move to and from each other based on the vibrations that we both emit.

Are those emotions of vibrations working within the Lord's orchestration?

How do we recognize His works?

The beauty of God's movements is recognizable if I continue with one accord to be able to recognize Him in all things pure.

Thy will be done on earth as it is in heaven

The earth is crying out in pain.

The axis of her hinges is off.

Elements move according to her breathing of tears that echo throughout the atmosphere.

The waters catch all her heavy droplets of pain from her eyes.

God orchestrates through the elements and movements of what is within.

Something that hinders my ability to operate in this world is used for God's will.

I am blind, but God sees through me.

He uses my eyes as though they are His.

My eyes are weak, but how am I still able to see?

It is only God that heals me.

I am humbled to be of service to You.

Sounds of the Wave

My truths to be unraveled
My untruths to be put far away from me
The sounds of the unsaid
The unsaid to not be heard
Quiet nothings screamed out loud
A whisper that gets louder
Breath after breath breathed
Sigh after sigh
My chest rises
Rises to the rhythm of my heart as it beats
My aliveness radiates
My truths to be said as the sound of the waves move continuously day by day
What truths? What sounds?
The truths of my heart
The sounds of my voice as I utter this syllable and that
To make a word, a sentence, a meaning to be said
The unsaid thoughts in my head
My head wraps around the words breathed in me

Surround Sound

The raindrops fall ever so lightly.
Feel wet drips from the sky.
Smell the fresh dew.
Hear the lightning and thundering utter surround sound.
Look up into the deep.
White flash of light, sometimes purple.
The birds chirp, flying through the individual drops of water.
Look down and see the rain spot the ground in a pattern that looks so random
that it is spaced perfectly from the next raindrop.
The water touches your face, while your clothing becomes soaked with
freshly made drops of water.
Thunder again and more rain.
Walk thru the water filled drops.
It is becoming of great form.
Droplets become fully prepared drops of dew that stain the environment
before it rinses away.
It vanished as if it were never there.
The proof was here, but now it is gone.
Begin again.
Surround sound.

I Fly Above Raging Waters

The waves are 20 feet tall. A horrible rage trying to engulf me in a torment. Torments of life and death. Will I survive through these currents of unknown waters? I am flying, looking down at the waves, but from up here, it is a beautiful sight. Water sprinkles on my face as I soar through the waters that rise from the raging waters. I am smiling at the sight and overwhelming feeling of peace. There are no thoughts in my head. Only the knowing that I am okay while I fly above raging waters. From this view I see the rage is only but a glimpse of the unknown. I look above me and see the baby blue sky with clouds positioned perfectly. I swoop down closer to the raging waves that lost its rage when I found peace. The waves are the orchestration of the Conductor. This is not about how easy it is. It is about how hard it is. The constant cycles of the ups and downs of the emotional ride during your spiritual journey. Running to God in excitement and joy because of His gifts to you. Lying in bed sad and upset, stomach hurting because of the sins you do. Standing in a corner angry with yourself and the world. Having emptiness fill your universe with an already empty atmosphere. How to free your mind from the pains that stop you from continuing to move forward and grow? There is no stopping. Being still and stopping have completely different meanings.

Everything has been stripped away. Think about having everything that pertains to who you are, and what makes you. Being reduced to nothing so that God can provide you with all. Being reduced to nothing so that you can experience being all things.

Sculpting the body

God will sculpt my unrighteous corruptible body into a righteous incorrupt-
ible body.

I am made in the image of God.

He will mold my current body into my new body when the time comes.

I am a shell waiting to be sculpted into a new creature in Christ.

Put your hands over my hands as I mold you.

See how I take my time to perfectly mold you into a new creature.

I press softly as not to damage your fragile body.

Each touch is a movement that I put much thought into, carefully molding you.

My fingers press on you with different pressures depending on the area that
I am sculpting.

Look at the Sculptor who sculpts clay into art.

You are my ultimate art.

I have carefully created you with Love.

I know you, now know me.

I am the clay of the earth that You have so elegantly put together.

I am the everlasting candle that You oil daily to keep lit for the world to see.

Your power and Your might Father.

I am the living water that You have gracefully and mercifully given me.

I am alive because of the breath that You have gratefully given me.

You are the light that keeps me together as I maneuver the pains and traps of
this world.

The Sculptor sculpts a masterpiece in me

His touch

To feel the Father through my fingers.

As soft as a father's touch to his infant.

My tears fall slowly down my cheeks.

Jesus uses His finger to carefully wipe the tears from my face.

One touch to my tear, then another, until the space He touches is not touched by a tear again.

My cheek is dry of tears.

The feel of knowing He is here when I do not see Him.

The ultimate joys of expression. More tears fall because of this.

Not from the sadness like before, but because I am happy.

I found what was always there, patiently wanting to hold me.

Right here with me. I remember the spot He wiped my tears away.

My tears stopped right there.

It is like He cupped His hand right there to catch every drop in His hand.

Filling up the palm of His hands with my tears.

When my tears touch that spot, they stopped falling because even my tears remembered His touch.

The boundaries of His touch remain even if those tears continuously fall down my cheek.

My thoughts were in that moment, freely expressing my emotions with little to say, but to speak with meaning.

The few words I could muster were filled completely up with gratitude, love, and joy.

To be filled with love that I felt my heartbeat with purpose.

My mind and my heart were one. I wanted to be in that space forever.

A feeling that I have never felt became an impression of time that came and gone.

That space of fulfilling joy and peace has returned at various times over the years, to be remembered for the remainder of my life.

Where are you?

I don't feel you as I did before.
I know you are here,
Yet I fear the invisible distance that appears.
The time and space you have given me is a gulf of air and lengths to grab
onto and pull You towards me.
Time and time again you allow me to find YOU LORD.
When You come O God, we will know.

Righteous Judgment

Who I am, I become.
To experience who I can be.
Wake up to see that I am me,
Continuing as the extended me.
I am all things, and all things are within.
It is what I release to become the true me.

I am who I am,
The dormant matters of my true essence rise as I am, and become who I am.
I always was sleep deep inside, waiting to burst thru the realities.
I am who I am, who meets who I am.

Nice to meet myself. I smile.
I was always there, even when the enemy tried to shred me.
Pulled me apart and teared at my heart.
Fingernails digging deep at my soul, to rip and detach all that contains me.

I can be all things; I was all things; and I am all things.
I knew courage, love, joy, expressions all in one.
I flew into the depths of freedom above
Knowing that I was safe and surrounded in God's love.

Silence

Oh,
The silence of silent
How it pierces through me
Like a nerve shocked into existence
That has become the deep pains of silence.

Don't You See?

What was I protecting myself from?
From the destructing forces that surrounded me.
I am voiceless.
You are my voice.
I am voiceless,
Don't you see?

Echo

The echo of voice in the halls
The echoes of silence in the halls
Still silence
Voice of laughter's
The echoes of echo
Year after year
From womb and back again
Daily
A constant cycle
A circular movement
That never ends
It keeps going around and around and around
The silence can be stilling
The still can be peaceful
Peaceful silence that bears the words never spoken
Yet we know their meanings
What meaning of a reason that's been kept secret?
To never know the words that have never been said
But to know the meanings
Deep within our heads

In the Void is a Silence

Silence.... It pierces through the air like a high pitch sound that hurts your ears... Shhhh, be quiet, be still. Do you hear that?

The stillness of words runs deeper than a single utterance of noise. On purpose or not, the silence is a piercing sound.

The unknown is stronger than the single letters that are brought together to make a word that connects one syllable to the following one.

The individual murmurings that scream, "I am here!" Silence.

Runs deeper than a bunch of ABCs.

Silence speaks. What is louder than words? What utters, "I am here and is heard?"

Nonverbal communications are disappearing with the voids of speaking as though there is something to be said.

Nothing is loud like a banging in my head that keeps me up.

Nothing is filling the void of wanting there to be something more than the silence that fills the air. Shhh...

The simple answer of silence is an answer that you and I can bear because the still quiet nothings of a breath of silence can fill the void with a stare.

I have been silenced way too long.

I have been told that my voice and opinions do not matter in the stare and the glare of the person looking at me.

For some reason I remembered and brought those childish thoughts into my adulthood.

Nobody told me to be quiet, but I see those same stares and glares in the faces looking back at me.

I am not scared, but something deep inside of me kept me voiceless.

This voiceless me is behind the voice of society.

My being has been reduced to my ability to respond and react to those around me.

I severed my connection to what has kept me chained.

I was born into the bonds of shackles already locked with the key hidden from my reaches.

Hidden from my mental grasp of what should be, disguised into what I imagined was best for me.

Bottled up and thrown into a flame unquenchable.

For me to get what is mine, I threw the everlasting waters on it and walked up to it.

I walked through the unquenchable heat to find the complete me.

Pieces of me were all over the place.

I have not even travelled to many places, and there is a piece of me torn and hidden everywhere.

To be continually poked at, only to strike back with a two-edged sword the Lord has given me.

The power is in the tongue.

My voice box is an extension that completes the sound as my bowels ring to the unheard telling me to listen.

My words are important.

What it appears to be

I have learned to be voiceless by learning it from you.

The silent sittings like I am not even there.

There were those attention grabbers that touched your eyes only to keep your voice there.

I learned to be quiet, to want a word or sentence to be said.

There were those quiet nothings and wishing of more meaning in my head.

I kept these with me into adulthood not understanding why I was stuck in the past.

It was because my mind would rewind the still memories that I wanted to last.

I became a lifetime of those still memories and moments of spending time together.

Those times became a positive and a negative effect on my recollections of how to be me and all that contains my being.

A child spending time with her father.

Who can deny the child's love it has for him?

Even if the love he gives is not merely what that child needs.

It is only a speck of that essence of what it takes to give so much love when he only has learned what love appears to be.

It is passed on from parent to child, to child, then child.

A constant cycle of less love learned, through an unending lesson of what is not real.

What is next?

I continue with my life.
But something is different.
The old me is no more, disappeared?
If only that were true.
The old me is still me, but I want to be more.
The inner me is in search of Father once more.
I want to be in His beauty for always.
Surrounded by His love daily.

Filling the void of loss

To fill that loss,
What does one do to fill the emptiness?
What does one buy to fill the emptiness?
For example, the loss of a husband/wife in divorce. There is no physical
death involved, but a death of one becoming two.
When both are one, there is a connection that is severed to become two
individuals, instead of one in Christ.

Hoarding.
How hard is it to clean your slate?
The ins and outs of the truest and deepest hate.
The hate that is your past, that fights and burns your guided path.

What I treasure is trash to you.

The lights and colors of the free hearted.
To not hold in the stress and pain.

Real sickness is this.

Hoarding is an example of a temporary filler of a hole.
A hole that is needing to be filled within the deepest waters of the chambers
of the heart.

Truth Hurts

The truth hurts
Even those you love the most
When you care for their feelings and how they will be hurt and painfully
soaking it in, disrupting their life.
The truth hurts
But to grow
We must face the truth
The fears
The sadness
The angers that we keep stuffed deep within us
Only to never let it go.
For the pain that we painfully enjoy because that is the only thing that has
made us feel alive.
That makes us feel like ourselves.

When our inner being is ripped away, it feels like death
We lose a part of our identity,
Of whom we are, and it hurts even more than the pains that we have held on
to from our childhood.

It is a loss that seems unbearable
It is a disconnection that opens us up to the fears and unknowns of tomorrow

Remember

Remember, I feel just like you do. The hurts and pain of this life work simultaneously with joy and happiness. The sun shines, moon illuminates, reflections of light to remember.

We are strangers. We are friends. We are one. No difference, the same. No wonderings remain.

The unknown is stronger than the wants and haves that every person fall asleep to, wanting to know each day intimately. The cycle of this and that brings us together like the cycle of life.

Feelings divide. Feelings bring together. The feeling of life is a cycle that turns around and comes back again like it forgot that it can never be gone from me. From us.

Remember. Reflections of what is and what was can soon be. The same for me as it is for you.

Remember, I feel just as you do.

Exploring the unexplored

I wonder if I am exploring the unexplored.
Am I searching for the inner me?
When I cry silently where no one hears me, am I finding my soul?
Am I looking for any missing pieces?
For if one believes they are whole, another piece that we need presents itself.
Knowing thyself requires constant attention.
The ability to search for your hidden self within you requires control once the hidden is found.
To be able to maturely accept what it is your feeling and handle it accordingly takes control and practice.
I can compose myself when realizing and then I can go deeper once I am alone with the time and space to find me.

When I was a child, I spoke as a child

My childhood molded me to become an adult who is ashamed because I allowed my childhood trauma to rule my actions, behaviors, and thoughts as an adult. My childhood came back around full circle as an adult. As an adult, I re-accepted those things that deeply cut and hurt my heart as a child. I allowed what once was, resurface and slowly kill me from the inside. I can say that I now really care for my insides. They have worked hard to keep me alive thus far. I worked against myself before I truly met Christ, but not anymore. "When I was a child, I spoke as a child, I understood as a child, I thought as a child: but when I became a man, I put away childish things" (1 Corinthians 13:11 NKJV). Now in the present, I am internally who I am as I am becoming who I will become. I am present in the pains I have accumulated those negative pressure ridden years of thoughts and emotions. My current health proves that to be. How I am internally is who I have grown to be as an adult in my now. The Lord begins to clean me up, beginning with the inner me.

I have been building on my foundation of Christ. I have read how to be mature in Christ. Now I must be mature in Christ. My perceptions and awareness have matured. I have made mistakes and regrets, but I release them and do not hold onto those feelings and emotions. However, I will never forget because they are for learning purposes and for my growth during this journey of mine. I have trained myself through practice to distinguish being good from evil. Well, Jesus trained me within my life experiences. Now is the time for me to strengthen what I have so that I do not lose what God has given me.

To become that child again was not as easy as it sounds.
I had to meet her all over again,
and feel all her emotions and feelings that she buried deep within her.
I had to make a connection with my inner childhood self that I disconnected
with a very long time ago in hopes to never meet her again.
To communicate with a scared, fearful, drained little me was hard.
Little me learned how to hide from those external pains by tearing apart
those feelings, emotions, and pains and placing them in their own separate,

and far from each other containers deep in my head and heart.
Fragmented pieces of wrong love and pains that I learned to keep with me into adulthood.
I hid those most hurtful memories deep within me, only to become them in my present.
I tore and ripped those pains and hurts I received as a child, only for them to resurface and hurt me some more as an adult.
I thought I ran away from my childhood, only to find out that I am still being chased.
I am still my little seven-year-old self.
I had to confront her.
I had to become her to remember those missing pieces that haunted me and separated me from the love of God.
I held her, rubbed her head goodnight, and kissed her wet cheek and she slept a sweet sleep.

I ripped it up

Why would you rip it up?
It only had a small tear.
Even though it is in small pieces, all over the floor, and in the trash,
I can pick up all the pieces and God will put it back together again.
Why rip up what is not yours?
Completely broken,
Torn like a piece of paper.
So weak and feeble,
Yet, strength resides in it each day.
My home,
My life,
My heart.

Heartbeat
There it goes again; do you hear it?
Did you see it move?
It did it again!
Even more now,
I put the torn pieces of paper back together,
Holding it waiting for a knock, a tick, a beat.
Anything God has in store for me.
It jumped, it moved! It beat.

Blood flowing

The flow goes up and back down,
And up again.
In and out and through again.
The flow moves fluid like it has done it before.
Time and time again,
And then no more.
No need for it, it's new.
The place it was, is an empty space that I will always remember.
A new heart.
Completely different.
It fell apart, broken to bits,
No feeling.
Put together, not glued, no surgery is needed.
It disappeared.
I don't feel it beat the same.
It's there, it's just new.

Breath,
My soul,
Your breath,
I'm whole.
A child, who's grown.
A woman, new fold.

The pressures of today

The stresses of tomorrow
Close your eyes
Breath
Be still
My body feels it all
The pain,
It suffers,
Release,
New life.
The energies,
go a fluttering,
recyclable,
Re-use.
Positivity surrounds me,
Just look.
Pick it up.
A beautiful flower waiting to be picked.
Many colors
Vibrant and moving.
Flying and floating
Like the wings of a butterfly.
Relax,
Just breath,
Mind still flows like still waters.
Naturally moving,
Is alive forever more.

Destiny

I feel the untouched stares
The glare of a wonder never seen
The rewinds and unwinds of the undone
The untouched
A mystery to be amazed
The help of a friend
As you complete your exciting runs and hides of a test and trial always meant
to pass
You feel the overwhelms, confusions, even the emotions never felt
To feel and see what has not before been seen
The pure and untouched energies of your destiny

Intangible

No coulda, shoulda, woulda's
Because I did
What is done is not undone
Etched and sketched
A memory to redo
The intangible is visible
Right in front of me
I touched the invisible
It's tangible
A reliable, pure source of the joys and happiness within
How to hold deep inside what is bursting?
The everlasting fire that burns
Alpha and omega will always be a part of me
The twists and turns of a wild ride
The ins and outs of a consuming journey that lights the sacred hidden
meanings of my questions finally answered by my God.

An unexplainable adventure

One that will always be remembered
Treasured
To revisit the journeys of the mind
Are a souls revitalized
I thank You for allowing me to see your timeless desires
Now when I say thy will be done
A deeper meaning will be
How to explain the unexplainable
To the selected questions
Chosen not at random
But only by divine
I'll know when to speak
I'll know how to speak
By your Holy Spirit
That lives in me
I thank you for showing me my abilities
The capabilities that have been painted over with a false conception of how I
was to be
I am all things
All things that I am
In me, in all, a completed me

Run

I am running in this darkness trying to get out.
Trying to get somewhere out of this darkness.
I run and I am lost.
I have stayed away from me because of influences, peer pressures, distrac-
tions, and stresses; but I was never really gone from me.
I had to find her all over again.
Now that I found me, I will not lose her again.
I am precious in the sight of the Lord.
Now that I understand that deep within me, I do not want to lose it again, ever.
So, I am going to work on it and strengthen what remains in hopes to dwell
with my Father in heaven on earth.

The Blahs and head grabs
of the beginning of inner growth

Whatever it is you think spiritual growth entails, you just might be wrong. How to explain the unexplainable? Most people do not even realize that they are currently in a process of growing. All they know is that they are in pain, which is the growing pain of maturing into a new creature in Christ. The growing pains of a fully grown person. How can that be? You thought you were done growing once you became an "Adult" at an "Adult age." NOOO. Mentally, you are still growing. The definition of being fully grown might not pertain to you. If we are constantly in an ever-changing state, how can we be fully grown? Are your decisions fully grown? Do you look fully grown? What does that really mean!?? It is a meaning that has proved meaningless when it comes to our spiritual growth that results in the deep and intense meanings of the person that you start to become in Christ.

Once you have reached maturity according to man's standards, I challenge you to reach maturity in Christ. It is not easy at all, but that is where the challenge comes in at. Instead of saying, I challenge you to do.

The flow and constant continuation of actions and reactions is a wave that remains moving. What you do, another person feels it. The impressions that I received as a child have had strong impressions in me as an adult. They continued in my internal memory for my whole life, only to be tried and retried for God to use me. I am used to being used by people. My decisions have been manipulated by those I know and do not know; the feelings of being taken advantage of by those around you. This has angered me. I got over it, and I get over it when I am in a situation that is similar. When you know you do not like the effects of it, but continue to allow such things to happen, ask yourself, why do I allow this to continue after I get hurt, even after I realize what is going on? Do you have the choice to say no and walk away? If you could walk away, would you? When I tell God, 'Thy will be done on earth as it is in heaven', I mean it. God can use me. When I want to do something, I pray that it is within Gods will and not my own. For God gives me my desires. I must work on what He gives me so that I can mature on this journey and become the woman and church God wills for me.

I wonder how much of who I am now has been manipulated by what is in the world. I wonder how much of one event that is completely different than me and my interactions are connected to me and my events? Jesus has been by me, holding my hand, letting me know that everything is okay. He asks me to trust Him as I journey with Him.

How much of too much will I accept in my life? For my mental, emotional, physical, and spiritual well-being, I will not accept negative that is for sure. I can only handle so much and becoming aware of my level of acceptance has been important in my journey. By not taking too much harm from others begins now. Not taking too much of what I do not like begins now. I ask, why do I take so much of some things and not of others? It might be the level of involvement. I do not give some people or events any of my energy because I already know that is what I will not deal with. For instance, there are those people who are negative, and I do not involve myself with them at all, unless I must have some level of involvement with them like at work. But through experience, I limit even those communications.

I learned that experiences come and go and may come back again in our lives. With whom we experience with will vary. The constant that remains the same is you. You are experiencing. To experience death and life at the same time, to be nothing and everything at the same time, to hate and love at the same time; what is the meaning of this? To put away with meaning and just be. This is when my will is for the Lords will. I am not of my own anymore, but Gods. My thoughts and behaviors are for Him, and I must remain in Him to receive His free gift of life. It is new and different, nothing that I would have ever imagined. Challenging is an understatement. Rewarding at its most. When your whole world ends and your new world begins, you can feel that with what is going on globally right now.

My personality is determined and can be determined only by me. The reality, the actualities of what I can be is the true me. Do not become obsessed with who you want to be, who you want to see, and who you want to read. I ask, should I remain sleep in a dream-filled world? Where my dreams become my reality and my reality becomes my dead-filled world. The twists and turns of the conscious, who wants to be unconscious, only to be re-conscious. Which is true? My one asked question that may have already been answered. To receive an answer to what I somewhere, deep inside, already know. Will I remember? The question asked has already been answered. I smile, a light, and them a glimmer. A shimmer of hope that I stop to remember to a time and space of openness. I hear, no I see and remember. You bring me back to where I am at momentarily. At this time and space, I remember where I am. I am all things, and all things are me because God has freed me from all the chains that have kept me locked down. I am all things because Yah is in me. Yah has changed me, by His spirit. For I was dead, but I am made alive. By His blood I am the beginning and the end.

The system of breaking the unhealthy habits in your life must be taken one day at a time. Each time you live in that bad habit or unhealthy moment, remember that, and continue. What were your thoughts before, during and after? After so amount of time, how have your thoughts changed? Pay attention if your thoughts have changed or adjusted any at all. It will take time and practice to master healthy habits. Change your habits and modify your thought process.